Talking to
Animals

Talking to
Animals

Gerald Bailey
Illustrated by John W Taylor

ELEMENT
CHILDREN'S BOOKS

SHAFTESBURY, DORSET · BOSTON, MASSACHUSETTS · MELBOURNE, VICTORIA

To Notchka and Cow

© Element Children's Books 1999
Text © Gerald Bailey 1999
Illustration © John W Taylor 1999

First published in Great Britain in 1999 by
Element Children's Books
Shaftesbury, Dorset SP7 8BP

Published in the USA in 1999 by
Element Books, Inc.
160 North Washington Street,
Boston MA 02114

Published in Australia in 1999 by
Element Books and distributed by
Penguin Australia Limited,
487 Maroondah Highway, Ringwood,
Victoria 3134

Reprinted March 1999

Cover design by Design Section
Cover photograph from the Image Bank
Typeset by Dorchester Typesetting Group Ltd.
Printed and bound in Great Britain by Creative Print and Design Wales,
Ebbw Vale

British Library Cataloguing in Publication data available.
Library of Congress Cataloging in Publication data available.

ISBN 1 901881 97 0

Contents

Introduction　　　　　　　　　　　　　　　　9

Chapter 1　A New Puppy　　　　　　　　13

Chapter 2　Dogs – Our Best Friends　　　22

Chapter 3　Sociable Wolves　　　　　　40

Chapter 4　Top Cats　　　　　　　　　53

Chapter 5　Whispering to Horses　　　　76

Chapter 6　Intelligence in the Sea　　　100

Chapter 7　Our Chimpanzee Cousins　　112

Chapter 8　Talking Is Good for You　　　121

Introduction

When you were very little, you did an amazing thing. You learned a complete spoken language. It seems a simple enough task, and it's something that we all take for granted. But learning that language helps us to do one of the most important things that humans must do if we are to get along with each other. It helps us to communicate.

Communication is the key to learning and to living with the other members of our society. We do not only use spoken language to communicate; we use other methods as well, such as sign language or the way we move our bodies, which is sometimes called body language. Even the way we behave helps us to communicate our thoughts and feelings.

When we think about communication, we usually think about it in terms of humans. We don't think about other animals, such as dogs or cats or even dolphins. But, just like humans, all animals communicate in some way or another, either with members of their own kind or with members of another species. They even have their own languages. This book is about communication among animals, both between themselves and with humans.

Our knowledge of the ways in which animals communicate helps us to understand them better. It also helps us to enjoy their company more. After all, many animals have inhabited our planet far longer than we have. We share our world with them, so we should try to understand as much about them as we can, especially the ones closest to us.

Thoughts and feelings

We often talk about the way we feel and think – our thoughts and emotions. But what about our animal friends, such as the dogs and cats that share our homes? Do they have thoughts and emotions too? Most people have been taught that they do not, that only humans experience such things. But dogs and cats are mammals, just like us. If we have developed the ability to have thoughts and emotions, why not other mammals?

Humans have developed thoughts and feelings because they help us to survive. If they did not, we wouldn't have these abilities. The same thing applies to our ability to learn and reason. Such things allow us to cope with a variety of problems. The same thing applies to other animals. It would be very short-sighted, and wrong, of us to think that only humans have these abilities.

Here is an example. When my dog Parsley first started to eat from a small bowl placed on the floor, the bowl would begin to shift along the floor as she energetically licked up the last of her meal. At first she began to follow it along until the last scrap of food had been finished. Before long, though, and without any help from me, she realized that if she placed one front paw on the dish it would not move. Now she could finish her meal without having to follow the little bowl along the floor. She had figured this out all on her own. It seems a simple thing. But for a young dog, not so simple!

The same thing applies to communication. The ability to think, feel, and reason has helped other animals to develop systems of communication, just as humans have developed their own systems. And in some cases, it would seem that a number of animals have an even more highly developed ability to communicate, especially over distances, than we have.

Here is a curious story about a group of dogs that seemed to have an almost magical way of communicating with their owner. Each day, just before the owner returned home from work, the dogs would walk down to the front gate and wait for him. They were never wrong about when he would arrive, and were always there waiting for him.

The owner could not work out how the dogs knew exactly when he was coming home. He suspected that either they guessed correctly at the right time, as it was more or less the same each day, or they could scent him or the car from some distance away. To find out the answer, he tried an experiment. Instead of leaving work at the usual time, he left very early. Then, rather than driving home in his car, he took a taxi. The route he took home was different as well, so that he arrived from a completely different direction. Imagine his surprise when, on cue, the dogs sauntered down to the gate and were there waiting for him when he arrived. How could the dogs have known when to expect him? He had arrived home at a completely different time of day, in a different car, and by a different route. What form of communication could they have used? The answer to that is not easy to discover. And we'll talk about it later on. For now, it must serve as a hint to show us that a dog's ability to communicate is certainly well developed.

A New Puppy

The sun was shining with a warm glow on the day we set off to collect our new dog, Parsley. We'd already named her Parsley in honor of the little lion in a famous television program. You see, Parsley was a Lhasa Apso, which means "little sentinel lion dog" in Tibetan, so it seemed an appropriate name. I say that Parsley is a Lhasa Apso, but she isn't quite. At least that's what her owner told us.

It all began about a week before, when we read in a national magazine that some puppies were for sale. But when we phoned the breeder the news was not good. All the Lhasa puppies had been sold. She could hear the disappointment in my voice. "We do have one other, though," she said. "It's from the same litter, but it isn't quite right. We call it a Prapso."

"A what?" I asked.

"Well, it's a kind of throwback. Every now and then one comes up in a litter. It goes back hundreds of years to the time when Lhasa Apsos, Tibetan terriers, and Chinese Pekinese were first being bred. They all come from the same original breed, you know.

"Anyway, a throwback has some of each breed in its make-up. Usually it ends up looking part Lhasa Apso with a bit of Pekinese thrown in. A throwback is smaller than the normal animal and doesn't grow the lovely long hair of true Lhasas. It still has longish hair with a beard and mane, but the hair is shorter than in the thoroughbred dogs. We call it Prapso because it's 'perhaps a Lhasa'."

The owner chuckled as I listened to her in silence. I thought that I'd heard of Prapsos before, but I wasn't sure. One thing I was sure about however – I knew I wanted the little dog that was not quite right, the little rogue Lhasa. What did I care if her hair was not as long as it should be? I wanted a companion and a friend, not a show dog. And Lhasas make excellent friends.

Getting ready

One week later everything was ready for the new arrival. We had a special box for the puppy to lie in, lined with an old torn sweater of mine. It smelled of me a bit too, which would help her to bond with me in future. We also chose some toys that were the right size for her to play with, including a glove puppet and an old sock tied in a knot so that she could play tug-of-war with it. We made sure we had enough supplies of proper puppy food and a bright red bowl that was just the right size for a puppy. We had also bought a normal collar and lead, and a second lead to fit with a harness around the puppy's body.

The drive to the breeder's kennels took us through pretty green valleys and tree-lined hills. Every now and again the Sun's rays would flood through the high trees, creating a curtain of sunlight. Although the landscape was very beautiful I could not stop thinking about the little rogue with whom we were about to spend many, many years. After all, this was an addition to our family. Not a toy, or something to be thrown out if it no longer pleased us. Parsley would be as much a part of our family as any other member – a fellow animal in a tiny society. Our family would be the same to her as the pack is to a single wolf.

But there was one big difference – she would always be dependent on us for food, warmth, and shelter. We could not let her down.

The first encounter

Mrs. Barker, the breeder, greeted us cheerily as we arrived at the kennels.

"You must be here for the Prapso," she said.

As she led us into the front room of her house, immediately we saw two Lhasa puppies playing behind a large green settee. They were lovely, like balls of fluff with noses and eyes. One was black with a white beard while the other was a steely gray. We watched the puppies at play for a few minutes before Mrs. Barker returned with what looked like a fur glove on her hand.

"Here she is!" she exclaimed.

We both looked at the little bundle that she held up, and our mouths seemed to drop open at the same time.

"Oh my goodness!" I cried.

Parsley was, without doubt, the cutest, most lovable puppy we had ever seen. She was a foxy reddish-brown color, with a white beard. Her huge brown eyes twinkled, and her tiny button nose twitched above the upside-down Y shape of her mouth.

We looked at each other and grinned as Mrs. Barker handed over our new companion.

"She may look like a Lhasa now," said Mrs. Barker, "but when she grows up her fur will be shorter. She'll still have the beard and full fur around her tail and feet, so she'll look OK."

"She looks just fine to us," I exclaimed.

We said good-bye to Mrs. Barker, and as we walked back to our car we tried to reassure Parsley that she was in good hands. So now began the communication process that would bond Parsley to us, her new parents, just as a wolf cub in the wild bonds to its pack.

New family, new pack

Parsley was obviously a bit frightened. She was leaving the only home she had known, as well as her mother. Still, at eight weeks old she was young enough to take everything in her stride as long as we treated her properly. In the car she snuggled up to my wife who had placed a sweater on her lap to make a

resting-place for the puppy. Parsley sniffed it at first, her little nose moving rapidly up and down, then snuggled into it.

She got used to the scent of us as we traveled and seemed to like being gently stroked. She even slept for a while. But when she woke she was disoriented and did not know where she was. We tried to reassure her as best we could. Then, to my wife's delight, this little creature began to burrow her way up the sleeve of my wife's coat. She was able to crawl all the way up its wide arms to the shoulder. When her head popped out at the top we both laughed. Parsley could sense the happiness as well. She seemed to smile, as dogs can do.

Home at last

When we arrived home, Parsley was carried on her bed into the house and placed immediately into the box that would be hers when she wanted it. She snuffled around trying to get the scent of the box and the sweater in it, then she decided she would explore for a bit, forgetting that she was hungry. She scurried into every nook and cranny, sniffing at anything she could reach with her nose.

Soon, tiredness overcame her and she

decided to go to sleep – not in her box, but just where her tiny legs finally gave in. She curled up into a tiny ball and was soon dozing peacefully. Very carefully, I picked her up and placed her in the box so she would begin to recognize that this was *her* place. The more of her scent there was in the box, the more she would accept it as her own sleeping place.

Bedtime for Parsley

That first night, when we went to bed, we wondered whether Parsley would accept being on her own in her own place, or whether she would want to be with the rest of her new family. After a few minutes we heard her crying and trying to scramble up the stairs to reach our bedroom. We had to make an instant decision. If Parsley was not allowed to be with us at night, we must ignore her cries and wait for her to settle down. It would take time, maybe days even, for Parsley, or any other puppy, to accept their place and feel comfortable on their own. Small puppies are very close to their mother and will follow her around. They will follow you in the same way. When you bring a new puppy home it will naturally want to follow you and be with you. If you do not want your dog to sleep close to you, you must let it get used to its new sleeping area, and being on its own, right away.

We found Parsley halfway up the staircase, hauling herself up each step as if she were a mountaineer. Needless to say we could not resist her and bundled her up, depositing her at the bottom of our bed. We assumed that she would be content to sleep there. In the morning we found her curled up between our pillows, sleeping peacefully!

CHAPTER 2

Dogs – Our Best Friends

In order to communicate successfully with your dog, or with any other animal, you have to understand languages other than your own spoken one. Your dog will learn to understand some of your language, but it is just as important that you understand its language as well. In fact, dogs communicate in a number of different ways, which include sound, scent, and body language. Each of these is important, and the more we understand them the better we will get on with our dog friends. As Parsley grew up and became one of the family, I learned so much about the way dogs communicate with us and with each other.

The "alpha" dog

In the wild, each pack of dogs has its leader, the so-called "alpha" animal. I had to take the role of the leader dog in Parsley's case. I had to become her "alpha" dog. This is what any dog owner must do to gain the respect and loyalty of their dog. You must let it know that it is a member of your family. With few exceptions, dogs are not loners. You must communicate to them that they now belong to a new pack, or social group. And you must communicate to them that you are the head of the pack. Your dog will soon communicate back that he or she understands its place in the group and is happy with it. Once the new dog knows its place it will want to please its pack leader – you. It will do as you tell it because it wants to, because it wants to please you. You can reinforce this by praising your dog when it does the right thing. And just watch its tail wag with delight!

Mimic muscles

You can usually tell how a person is feeling by looking at their face. Even the eyes can give away whether they are feeling sad or happy. We don't usually consider that the same thing applies to dogs. But dogs, just like humans, are able to use their faces to communicate feelings. This use of facial expression is a form of body language.

Unlike many other animals, dogs can change their facial expression to show how they feel. This is because a dog has a well-developed set of "mimic" muscles in its face. By using these muscles, a dog can tell you if it is angry or afraid, pleased or unhappy.

When Parsley first arrived, it was a delight to watch her face light up and her eyes shine when she was pleased. Now she seems to smile when she is happy. We also learned that a drooping face and dull eyes meant that she was unhappy about something.

Dogs can grow tired and irritable just as people can, and it often shows in their faces. It is best to leave them alone when they are in this kind of mood. Sometimes dogs use a direct stare, with the face set still and the eyes piercing like daggers. This is a threat, and it is meant to warn you, or an enemy, to stand off. (The same kind of facial expression is used by wolves in the wild – *see page 47.*)

"Tickle my tummy"

When Parsley comes to greet me she often jumps up on the sofa and rolls onto her back,

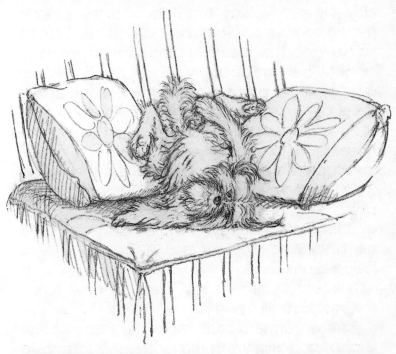

exposing her tummy. She is asking me to tickle or stroke it. Many dogs like this kind of soothing touch, but why?

Rolling over and exposing its tummy is a dog's way of saying that it recognizes you as the superior "alpha" dog and is glad to be part of your pack. It is a submissive position that dogs also adopt when they have been naughty. Until she accepted that it was the wrong thing to do, Parsley would often walk down the driveway that leads to the lane in front of our house. The lane can be busy, so it is not a good place for Parsley to be roaming about. She would saunter down the drive from time to time, pretending that I was either not there or not looking at her. Every now and then she would stop and look back toward the house, just to see how I was going to react. Inevitably I'd wait to see how far she would walk, and then go and fetch her. At that point, seeing my stern face and anticipating a telling-off, Parsley would roll over onto her back and stick her legs in the air. She was being submissive.

"Naughty girl!" I'd say, thinking how funny she looked and trying to sound angry.

Parsley understood that she had done wrong, and was using this body language as a way of apologizing.

Fear

When dogs are afraid, their heads bow down and their tails curl down between their legs. Usually they turn and try to skulk away when adopting this form of body language. It is called cowering, and it is not a pleasant sight to see. Dogs cower when they feel threatened, sometimes even if no threat is intended. Dogs that have been repeatedly hit by their owner, for instance, will cower if they see a raised hand, no matter what the raised hand is for. Sometimes when a dog is adopted from the kennels of an animal rescue organization, the new owner may see the dog cower for no apparent reason. Usually this means that the dog has been mistreated in some way.

In this situation, you have to try and find out all you can about what scares your dog and then try to "reprogram" its reactions to certain actions. In other words, you have to create a new set of communication signals with the dog, so that it understands that a raised hand does not mean it is going to be struck. It might mean, for instance, that you are going to reach up to the top shelf for a treat for your dog. Try to make your own body language communicate something good, not something bad or threatening.

Standing tall

Some dogs have long tails, others have quite short ones. Some tails curl, like Parsley's, while others are straight. Whatever the shape or length of its tail, a dog wags it to show us how it feels. Usually a brisk wag of the tail means that the dog is happy, perhaps to see you arrive home, or perhaps because its long-overdue dinner is finally ready. Dogs also wag their tails when they are happy to see other dogs – the ones that they like, that is. They make an altogether different movement, however, when they meet a dog that they don't like or are afraid of. The tail is immediately placed between the legs. This is a sign to the other dog, telling it "I am submissive, please don't attack me. I'm not going to attack you." This behavior will usually prevent a skirmish from starting.

Some dogs are very clever at communicating what they want another dog to think, even if it is not quite true. According to one story, a certain dog often went for walks by itself and usually had to pass a house where a much bigger, gruff mountain dog lived. The mountain dog considered that it was king of all it surveyed, and it would bark at any other animal that came close. All, that is, except this certain dog on its walk. The owner often wondered why there was never a row between these two dogs, so she decided to see what went on when her dog passed the gate where the mountain dog held court. What she saw was fascinating. Her small dog, rather than looking weak and submissive, stood as tall and

as proud as it could and trotted in a dignified manner past the gate and the mountain dog. Not a single bark was heard. Apparently the smaller dog's body language was signaling that it was a very dominant dog indeed. These signals were so strong that the mountain dog did not question them. It was a wonderful piece of deception on the part of the smaller dog, and shows just how well body language can work, even for animals.

The language of smell
Whenever Parsley finds something new, she

29

sniffs it first to see what smells, or scents, it gives off. If she is handed food, she will always sniff it first before eating it. To Parsley, and to any other dog, the ability to smell is as important as the ability to see or to hear. Scent is very important to dogs, and in some ways it is even more important than sight.

Dogs use scent to communicate, to find food, and as a way of examining something. Humans generally use sight to examine things, but a dog can find out as much about something by the scent it gives off as by the way it looks. This is particularly true when meeting other dogs. The scents that another dog carries tell a lot about the dog and where it has been. This is why dogs always seem to sniff each other when they meet. They can communicate many things to each other by scent.

A dog's sense of smell is much keener than ours, and a dog can smell specific things from a great distance. I'm sure Parsley can smell her favorite sliced chicken from at least a mile away! This sense of smell is important not only for examining things, but also for communicating. Every time you come back into the house your dog will greet you by sniffing around you. Without knowing it, you are telling the dog where you have been and what you might have been doing.

Your dog can pick up the scents of many things on your hands and clothes. It can even sense, it would seem, an event such as the birth of a new baby. In her book *The Hidden Life of Dogs*, the writer Elizabeth Thomas tells of returning home after visiting a newborn baby. Her dogs smelled her hands as usual. The odours they found on them made the animals oddly joyful. It was as if they knew that a happy event – a birth – had taken place, and it pleased them. Perhaps they could smell the newborn baby on Elizabeth's hands and immediately knew what the scent meant. Dogs are able to pick up the very faintest of scents, far fainter than any human can detect.

Greetings

When Parsley has been out on her own, she always greets our other dog, Cow, by sniffing around Cow's nose and muzzle. This is a way of giving off scent as well as receiving it. It is a kind of affectionate "hello," similar to a hug between two people.

When two or more dogs live together, they tend to pay more attention to an "outsider" dog that has just arrived – perhaps returning

from some kind of adventure. The home dogs investigate the other dog, checking all the scents that it carries. They investigate the different scents of its body, which may tell them what mood it is in, how tired it is, and how well it is. They investigate the dog's fur to pick up the scents of the places it has visited. They also smell its lips and shoulders, as well as its legs and feet. The scents they pick up communicate a lot about the dog's state and where it has been, without having to use any spoken language. We humans have lost much of our ability to communicate without the use of speech, yet our dogs can learn much about us when they sniff us on our return from somewhere interesting.

Toilet training

Like all puppies, Parsley had to be gently toilet trained. I knew that this would not take long, though. If there had been other dogs in the household at that time, left to their own devices they would have trained Parsley. Like all animals, dogs are basically clean creatures. Young dogs will quickly learn from the older dogs where they must go and where they must not go.

When Parsley went to the toilet in the wrong place, I showed her what she had done, then took her and placed her on the paper that I had put down in the outer room leading to our back garden. If I had wanted her to go outside, I would have taken her outside right away. I would do this later. It did not take many days until Parsley began to use the paper as her toilet. If she made a mistake, I gently scolded her, so she knew that she was wrong, then placed her on the paper again. At first, when she went in the right place, I praised her and made her feel that she had done the right thing and that it had pleased me. At no time did I need to hit Parsley to discipline her. Using violence to "train" a dog is both unnecessary and cruel. When you communicate your feelings to your dog it will learn and react because it wants to, not because it is afraid of the violent consequences if it does not. This is very important, and it is based on the ancient pack instincts of the dog.

When strangers meet

We live in a fairly isolated spot, so Parsley does not meet many strange dogs. But every now and then, one appears walking along the lane with its owner. When Parsley sees the dog, she performs a sort of ritual with it. On first sighting

the other dog, she dashes toward it as fast as she can. Then, a few yards away, she stops and looks straight at it with her head held high and her tail pointing up like a flagpole. After this pause, she continues toward the stranger. If it is a larger dog, which it usually is, she leaps up playfully at its side, then tears off hoping that the dog will follow her. If it does, she runs and circles it until it is close, and then she either leaps at it again or immediately lies on her back with her tail between her legs.

This kind of ritual may seem meaningless to us, or perhaps just a bit of playful fun. But to the dogs it has meaning, and it is used to sort out which is the superior dog. Dogs need their pecking order, or hierarchy, and when Parsley lies on her back she is telling the other dog that she accepts it as the superior one. If she remains with her head and tail held high, she has not. Instead, she feels herself to be superior. As most dogs are bigger than Parsley, she does a lot of lying on her back!

A voice language

When Parsley is in desperation, she makes a sound almost like a whine. This is part of her version of voice language, and it works very well. Probably all Lhasas use it, particularly when communicating with other dogs of the same species. What it tells me is that dogs, such as Parsley, can use their limited vocal abilities to "speak" to humans. It is up to us to take the time and effort to understand what the dog is saying. After all, we expect our dogs to understand the words we use to tell them to "sit" or "heel" or whatever.

The mother of Cow, our true Lhasa, was called Notchka, and Notchka must have had a lot of wolf ways left in her. When she reached full size I was always amused by her own special greeting. She would raise her head and give a long throaty howl, just as if she were singing to me. She reacted like a wolf in the wild greeting its pack-mate. Yet Notchka was greeting me, a human, with a howl. Sometimes I would howl back, just to please her.

When Cow was born, the greeting became even more fun. Notchka would begin howling, and then Cow would join in. They would howl along together for a while until they were sure they had offered a good enough greeting. It was marvelous to hear, even if it often made me laugh out loud. This was real communication between human and dog, both understanding what the language was and what it meant. Strangely enough, Parsley has never howled. And now that Notchka has gone, Cow hardly does it any more.

Elizabeth Thomas tells of a time when one of her dogs had to be put to sleep. The other dogs spent that night howling together. No one can know what the howling actually meant. But the dogs must have understood, through Elizabeth, what had happened. Perhaps they could scent something about her. Perhaps they were sad and comforting themselves, or perhaps they were howling to their lost friend.

Warning woof

Many dogs are bred to do specific jobs, for example sheepdogs or retrievers. Even though they are classified as "toy dogs," Lhasa Apsos originally had a very important job to do. Despite their small size, they were guard dogs!

Inside the aristocratic houses of Tibet, nestling in the great Himalayan Mountains, the Lhasa Apso was used as a sentinel, or guard, dog. A huge and fearsome Tibetan Mastiff stood outside the house to intimidate any would-be intruders, but it was up to the Lhasa to sound the alarm if any members of the household were in danger. It did this (and still does it today) by woofing in a deep meaningful way. The Lhasa's woof is part of its language of communication and is quite different to a normal bark. Lhasas do bark of course, but barking has a different meaning. Parsley will use her woof if she is not sure of someone, or something, approaching the house. If she knows who or what it is, she will either leave it alone or bark. This wonderful means of communication ensures that I always feel safe. Parsley has never been wrong.

"Back soon"

When Parsley first arrived, we never left her alone for very long. Sometimes we had to, of course, but she did have the company of our three cats. When we went out, we would always say "Won't be long, back soon, Parsley." At first she wanted to come with us, thinking she might be going for a walk. But she soon learned that these words meant we were going out and she had to stay behind.

She also knows that "going for a walk" means just that. When I first wanted her to stay still on a walk I would say "wait." I don't think I ever consciously wanted Parsley to react to that word rather than to "stop," or "heel," but it was the one that she reacted to. The reason she did so, of course, is that I used it repeatedly to mean the same thing. This is how dogs learn human voice language. It doesn't really matter which word or words you use, as long as they always mean the same thing and are used often. Your dog will soon get the message. After all, that's how we humans learn our own language.

- Dogs can express their feelings by smiling or staring angrily.
- When a dog rolls over to have its tummy tickled, it is saying that you are superior to it.
- A dog with its head and tail held high is saying "I'm the boss."
- A frightened dog bows its head and lowers its tail.
- When you return home, your scent tells your dog where you've been and what you've been doing.
- A whining dog is an unhappy dog.
- When you use the same words over and over again to mean the same thing, your dog will soon get the message of what you are trying to say!

CHAPTER 3

Sociable Wolves

Much of Parsley's behavior, and the behavior of dogs in general, is related to their wolf ancestry, or background. We can learn a lot about dogs by studying wolves. After all, every single breed of dog is a descendant of the wolf. For example, like their wolf ancestors dogs howl and arrange themselves into hierarchies.

Wolves often have a fairly bad press, being depicted as mean and evil. There are all sorts of stories about bad wolves, ranging from "Little Red Riding Hood" and "The Three Little Pigs" to frightening werewolf tales. Werewolf stories probably began in central Europe at a time when wolves roamed the land much more freely. Yet wolves are not bad or evil at all. In fact, they are very sociable, family animals that live in closely knit social groups called packs.

Alphas and others

Wolves generally belong to a pack of 8–10 animals, sometimes more. People who study wolves refer to the pack's head wolf as the "alpha" wolf. The alpha wolf is usually the oldest wolf and is always male. His mate is the alpha female and second to him. Their children are next in the order of the pack, and their grandchildren or weaker wolves lower down still. There is always a ladder-like hierarchy among wolves, just as there is among dogs.

Wolves live in a tightly knit society and must know their place within that society. This means that they have to be very good communicators – and they are. Wolves use body language, scent, and sound to make themselves understood by other members of the group. We can see how important communication is when we understand how hard life would be in the wild without it.

One-litter families

The most important things in a wolf's life are finding food and making sure there are more wolves to carry on the family. Food is usually scarce, so generally only one litter at a time is born into a pack. The alpha female will try to stop a young female from becoming pregnant. Usually, she can do this by just staring the younger female away from any encounter with a male. A look from the head female is enough, but younger wolves can also be made to feel very uncomfortable and ill at ease by a female that is already pregnant (and usually in a bad mood). This may seem cruel, but it is not. The wolves know that there is only so much food to go around. If two litters are born into a pack, there will probably not be enough for any of the young and so all the newborn wolves might die. If only one litter is born and all the other wolves help out by finding food and "babysitting," then there is a good chance that the pups will survive the long winter ahead.

Wolf play

As wolf pups grow, they learn to play in a rough-and-tumble way, hitting each other with their paws and making mock attacks. They watch their parents and the other wolves in the pack carefully and learn from them. Although domestic animals, dogs do the same thing if given a chance. By playing in this way the wolves will establish their own little hierarchy,

with the strongest and boldest pup at the top. This is important, because one day he may have to lead the pack.

Status

There are many reasons why animals need high status, or rank, but for wolves such high rank can be a matter of life or death. This is true not just for the adult wolf but for its offspring as well. Among wolves, and dogs too, high-ranking males are more likely to be selected as fathers by females wanting to mate. A high-ranking female is more likely to have a litter and to keep it. Wolves know this, and it seems that dogs who are given a choice know it as well. Lower-ranking wolves do not try to take over as alphas unless they are very strong and able. This makes sure the alpha is always a good leader.

Hunting wolves

When they are old enough, wolf pups will learn to hunt. Communication between wolves makes hunting much easier. After all, many of the animals that a wolf must prey on to survive, such as caribou and elk, are bigger than the wolf itself.

Wolves have to be clever and tireless in the hunt, and often have to hunt in packs. When the hunt begins, the wolves greet each other by howling. The howling not only calls the pack members together but warns other wolves that they should beware. Other packs usually respect this because they do not want to fight over territory – life is hard enough! The wolves then move out and roam their territory until they find prey.

When wolves find the right animal, they move in on it down wind – that is, in the direction from which the wind is coming. This prevents the animal from picking up the wolves' scent. When they get close to their prey, the wolves creep forward silently. Sometimes they move in single file until they are

close enough to begin the chase. Finally, they charge after the prey animal and lunge at it. The victim must be killed with the wolf's jaws, so the attacker must aim accurately at the animal's neck.

Music of the night

Wolves howl in order to communicate by sound. Only dogs bark. Sometimes two wolves will howl together in unison just for the fun of it.

People who have listened believe that the "tunes" they sing are purposeful. They don't just howl at any old thing. Perhaps they are communicating with each other, or just enjoying a good sing-song. At any rate, the wolves seem to gain great pleasure from doing it.

Wolves, like dogs, make a variety of sounds. They can howl, quaver, whine, grunt, growl, yip, bark, and wail. Each of these sounds has its own special meaning in the process of communication between animals, as well as between animals and humans. The Yupic people, who live in the Yukon River delta of Alaska, North America, claim they can understand wolves as easily as other people understand their dogs. Other Inuit people from North America rely on wolves to tell them when the caribou herds are moving. Caribou are as important to the Inuit as they are to the wolves; they provide the Inuit with meat as well as fur and skins to protect them from the cold. The Inuit also learn from the wolves where the caribou herds are located and in which direction they are moving. The Inuit maintain that the wolves set up a kind of com-munications network, rather like a telegraph system, passing messages from one pack to another for miles in advance of the caribou migration. The most interesting feature of this message system is that the sounds the wolves use are quite different from any other sounds they make.

Eye contact

As well as using sounds, wolves communicate with each other by sight. We know how a top female can use eye contact to intimidate her inferiors. An alpha male can use his eye contact just as effectively. In this way he can control his subordinates, the rest of the pack,

from a considerable distance. If he stares at a lower-ranked wolf intently, with a kind of glare, the lesser wolf will take on a submissive position by lying down or crouching, sometimes even with its tummy facing up. At other times, it will drop its head and tail and turn sideways or face away from the alpha wolf, just like a child that has been told off. It is possible to communicate with a dog in this way, although it can be difficult. Your dog won't be used to you using this type of communication and may not understand it right away.

The writer Elizabeth Thomas spent some time watching wolves on Baffin Island, in northern Canada. She tells how a young wolf and its mother were the first to notice her, and how they returned to their den almost immediately and began to howl. They were calling in other members of the pack that were out hunting. Soon the whole pack was howling together. Perhaps they were trying to tell the intruder that this was their territory and that she should move away. The wolves had apparently called an assembly, and they were being warned to stay away from the human. In fact this is exactly what happened. As a result, the wolves never again visited the place where they had spotted Elizabeth.

Dens for homes

A wolf's home is the den, which is often a hole dug into the side of a hill with a chamber at the end for sleeping and rearing cubs. The wolves on Baffin Island had a series of five dens that they used alternately each year, probably as a means of flea control. The dens were located along a river system and were reached by a trail that was so old the stone had been worn down to form a slight hollow. The wearing of the stone showed that the wolves, incredibly, had been using the same trail for thousands of years!

The den itself had probably been re-dug many times but it was always in the same hill. Clearly this was an excellent spot for the wolves' home. It was located about halfway between the winter grounds and the summer grounds of a herd of caribou, and so it was always within a few days' reach of good hunting. Also, the pups were born at around the same time that the caribou passed by the hill on their way to summer pastures. Then, in the fall, when the growing pups would be hungry, the caribou would pass back again heading toward their winter grounds. In addition, the hill made an excellent look-out and was near water. In all, the clever wolves had made a fine choice of location.

"Babysitting"

Most wolves spend the day hunting, either on their own or with the pack. But when a new litter of pups has arrived, one adult has to stay behind and act as "babysitter," since the pups' mother will have joined the hunting party. Young wolves are more or less helpless. They cannot find food for themselves and might become a meal for some other hunting animal if left alone for long.

Following some unspoken rule, the wolves take it in turn to watch the pups. The wolves that Elizabeth Thomas watched would hunt non-stop, while one stayed behind as babysitter. When a wolf returned from the hunt, the pups would rush out of the den and mob it. Then the wolf would lower its head, arch its back, and throw up a pile of chopped meat for the pups to eat. The mother, who was the head female, would sometimes throw up a second lot which she might have been keeping for herself. The returning mother would then take the place of the babysitter, but would usually go to sleep with exhaustion after the hunt – even though the youngsters might pester her to play. The babysitter would leave the den and join the others in the never-ending search for food.

A wolf's life is hard. Food is often scarce, and the climate can be terrible, with freezing temperatures and howling icy winds. But the patterns of communication that wolves have developed among themselves have enabled them to exist and thrive in the wilderness for thousands of years. They are truly wonderful animals and certainly don't deserve the bad treatment they have had from humans. So next time you look at your dog, remember there is still a wolf lurking in it somewhere. And spare a thought for the brave and skillful wolves that still roam the wild.

WHAT DO YOU KNOW?

- Every pack is headed by an alpha wolf, usually the oldest male.
- A top wolf will communicate its displeasure or anger to a less important wolf by staring or glaring at it.
- Wolves sometimes howl together in unison – just for fun!
- Messages about the movements of caribou herds are passed from one wolf pack to another.
- While their mother is out hunting, wolf pups are looked after by a "babysitter" from the pack.

CHAPTER 4

Top Cats

Humans are not the only animals that Parsley has to deal with in our household. We have three cats. At first we wondered how they would get along, but we need not have concerned ourselves. They get along very well. In fact, Parsley, being in her mind the superior animal, often acts as a mother cat, cleaning

the cats' ears and anything else that needs tidying up. She chases them as well, of course, because that's fun. And the cats seem to enjoy it too, since they often provoke Parsley into a chase.

When Parsley was a puppy, I often watched the cats and her together. I soon began to learn more about how cats communicate, with other cats, with dogs, and, of course, with humans.

Making friends

As a new arrival into the household, Parsley had to meet the three cats that lived indoors with us as well as the four that lived outside. I knew, though, that they would all learn to live happily together. People are often surprised that dogs and cats can live in the same family. However, they seem to get along together quite naturally. They are both carnivores, so one is not the prey of the other, and there is no competition for food since both kinds of animal are fed well. Still, cats are different and have their particular cat ways, even when it comes to communication. After all, dogs can't purr! Like dogs, though, cats also use scent, body language, and sound to communicate.

Miaow language

The cat language to which we are most attuned is its sound language – its miaow. Scientists think that cats can make more than 60 different sounds, from a purr to a loud wail. These sounds have different meanings depending on the cat's situation. A miaow can be a friendly greeting or a kind of inquisitive, curious chirrup. It can also signal hunger, fear, or loneliness.

Alexandra Sellers, an American author and cat lover, claims she has learned cat language. She actually reads books written in it to her cats! Her guess is that there are as many as 1,000 different miaows, each with its own meaning. I'm not sure she's right, but it would be wonderful if she was!

Purrfection

Cats use their purr to communicate different things. The only male, or tom, cat in our family has a particularly fine purr. It sounds like an outboard motor when he is in full flow. He usually purrs to tell us that he is happy, such as when he smells food or when he is stroked. Like all cats, he uses his purr to communicate other feelings as well. We know that cats purr when in great pain or in distress. What does the purr actually mean? It is probably a social signal to say that the cat is in a friendly mood. If a cat is injured, for instance, it may be signaling that it needs friendship and help. Cats also purr when they want something, signaling that I am happy with your company now and won't lash out at you, so please give me something to eat!

Purring first occurs when tiny kittens begin to feed from their mother. The kitten's purring lets the mother know that the kitten is reaching the milk and is content. At the same time, the mother will purr to show that she too is happy and relaxed. The purr of the kitten lets her know that nothing is wrong even if she can't see her offspring buried in the fur below.

Cats are two-way purrers. They purr as they

breathe out and as they breathe in. Big cats, such as lions and tigers, are one-way purrers. They only purr as they breathe outward, and it's a more spluttery purr as well. Still, big cats can do something that small cats cannot do. They can roar! Roaring is used as a warning to other big cats, or to any potential enemies, to stay away. It is very frightening to humans – and rightly so. After all, no one in their right mind would stand close to a roaring lion.

To little Parsley, our cats must have looked as lions might look to us, so she was a bit wary of them at first. The cats, on the other hand, did not seem to give a hoot about her. To them, she was nothing more than a troublesome infant, to be struck on the nose if she got out of hand. But how did the cats see us humans?

"Mother cats"

Quite simply, cats view us as big "mother cats." Mother cats feed, clean, and protect their children, and that is exactly what we do to our pet cats. In its mind, a cat remains partly a kitten all its life, with its human companion as the mother. You can see this in some of the ways that it communicates with us, and that we communicate with it. For instance, cats like to be stroked and they often come up to us, pushing and looking lovingly up at us until we respond. This is because the stroking movements we make on a cat's fur feel just like the licking movements of a mother cat. Kittens are constantly licked by their mother from the time they are born. Our hands acts like a huge tongue, doing the same job of "cleaning" and soothing.

When they are being stroked, cats often give a signal that goes back to their kitten days. They stick their tails straight up in the air. This is a signal that they are ready to be cleaned under their tail. They also do this when they are greeting other cats or humans whom they are pleased to see. Now that Parsley is one of the family, the cats often greet her in the same way. They certainly rub against her as they do against my legs when they want something to eat. Unfortunately for them, Parsley hasn't yet learned to open a tin of their favorite food!

A friendly face

As well as rubbing against you, a cat has another way of reacting when you offer it a greeting, or approach it when it has been asleep. In its rather graceful, laid-back way the cat will roll over onto its back and stretch out its legs, while yawning and twitching the end of its tail. This behavior is a cat at its friendliest, and it is reserved for its closest companions only. Cats would not risk this kind of behavior if they thought they were in any danger. With its tummy facing up, a cat is making itself very vulnerable. It is communicating to you that it really likes you and trusts you.

But be careful of one thing. When a cat behaves like this it is normally in quite a sleepy state. It seems to be offering its tummy to be tickled. Although it might allow this to happen, a cat's tummy is usually very well protected and you might receive a smart smack if you try to touch it. Cats generally find being touched there unpleasant, unlike dogs who love it.

Scent signals

Scent is a very important part of a cat's communication. When your cat says hello by rubbing against you, it usually goes through a very precise ritual. It begins by pressing its head or the side of its face against you. Then it rubs all the way down its side and finally twines its tail around you. If you reach down and begin to stroke it, the cat rubs harder, pushing the side of its face and mouth against your hand.

All these movements have a special purpose. In fact, the cat is going through a scent exchange between itself and you. A cat has special scent glands on its temples, at the corners of its mouth, and at the base of its tail. When it rubs against you, it is marking you with the scent from these glands. It is also picking up scent from you by rubbing its side against you. When a cat has finished doing this, it will walk off and lick its side to take in your scent.

To make a lasting relationship with a cat it is important that you allow this scent exchange to take place. It makes the cat feel welcome and part of the family.

Sadly, our noses are no longer good enough to pick up a cat's delicate scent, so we don't notice that it exists. But the cat does, and that's what is important.

60

Going for a walk

Unlike dogs, cats are not pack animals. They are very much individuals who like to do their own thing. When cats leave the house, they become virtually wild animals again, enjoying the outdoors and hunting, both of which they tend to do on their own. Cats don't form groups, or packs, and so they don't have the same need as dogs to establish rank or status. All cats think they are top cat! This is why you don't put a cat on a leash and take it for a walk. It just isn't interested. Nor will it try to please you because it thinks you are a higher-status head cat. So cats aren't taught to walk or heel or come when they are called. And you've probably noticed there aren't any sheep cats either!

You can imagine my surprise, then, when our cats began to act in a decidedly uncatlike way. Every morning I take Parsley for a walk down a private lane to the farm at the bottom. It's a pleasant walk with lots of grassy areas and things to smell. Soon after starting this morning ritual, I noticed that one or two of the cats would follow us for part of the way. In time, they began to come all the way down to the farm and back up again. Pretty soon, most of the cats joined in the walk down to the farm and back, coming along with Parsley and returning with her when I called her to come. The cats were coming for a walk, just as dogs do! But why? The answer may have something to do with the fact that I feed them and that they are looking for food. But they come whether they have been fed or not. So I guess that they just enjoy the walk. I certainly do, although I've had some queer looks from the odd person passing by!

Head to head

One of our outdoor cats is as black as coal, with no other coloring at all except a tiny fleck of white on her chest. She is called simply Black Cat. Like the other cats, Black Cat often comes for a walk. But she doesn't behave quite like the others. She likes to be carried! When we are about ten yards down the lane, Black Cat will reach up with her front paws and wait to be lifted up onto my shoulders. If I don't lift her she'll try to make her own way up, which can be quite painful. Once on my shoulder, she crawls from one shoulder to the other constantly nuzzling my face. This is a real show of affection, I thought. It is, of course, but there is a reason for it.

Cats communicate their greetings to each other, and to Parsley, by gently rubbing faces with each other. They cannot do this with humans, though, because we are too tall. Nevertheless, it is natural for them to aim their greeting at the head, and so cats will sometimes perform a little hopping movement on their back legs, aiming their head up at yours, just to show willing. This movement often begins when they are kittens and can't quite reach their mother's face.

Black Cat was simply greeting me in the best way she knew, head to head, just as she'd do with another cat. She wasn't content with my hand or the side of my leg. So for much of the walk she'd either greet me or happily sit on my shoulder as we walked along. When we returned and the walk was over she'd immediately jump down without any instructions from me. Like the other rubbing activity, the head-to-head contact is a way of mingling personal scents and creating a closer friendship or bond.

Scenting the furniture

How many times have you scolded your cat for scratching a favorite chair or settee? Usually the cat is told in no uncertain terms to go and scratch something else. We assume that the cat is scratching the furniture in order to sharpen its claws, and that it would be better off using the scratching post we bought for it, or even a convenient tree. In fact, the cat is really stripping off the worn-out sheath of its claws, just as a snake strips off its old skin. Underneath the old sheath is a brand-new, razor-sharp claw. Claw sheaths from the back paws are removed by chewing them away. A cat also scratches at furniture to exercise and strengthen the parts that cause the claws to protrude and then retract. These parts must be looked after, as they are vital for catching prey, climbing, and fighting rival cats.

There is another reason why cats do what seems to be a destructive job on your favorite household fabric. They do it to scent-mark the area. A cat has scent glands on the underside of its front paws. These are rubbed very hard against the fabric of the furniture being clawed. The rhythmic motion of the cat's paws squeezes scent from these glands onto the fabric and rubs it in, creating a scent print that says "this is mine."

The cat is also adding its scent to your scent. So it's often your favorite chair that gets mauled, time and time again. So don't be surprised if your cat ignores the things you want it to scratch and returns to its favorite place once more. It's really just being friendly.

Milk-treading

Often when I am sitting down and relaxing, one of our cats will jump up on me and begin to knead my lap slowly. Very often I can feel the tips of its claws beginning to nip as well, which is not always comfortable. Usually I try to stay still, rather than shunt the cat onto the floor or the closest chair.

This kneading action goes back to kitten-hood, when the tiny animal was taking milk from its mother's nipple. When a mother cat is lying relaxed and with her tummy exposed, the kitten knows that it might be time for a meal. The action of pushing and kneading, called milk-treading, stimulates the flow of milk for the kitten to drink. This is very satisfying for a hungry kitten.

When a cat performs a similar action on you, it is taking on its kitten life again, with you as the relaxed mother cat. It is a kind of soft, loving behavior that must be a bit like a cuddle. The problem is, the cat won't understand if one moment you are a kindly mother cat offering milk and the next you are pushing it off onto the floor. A real mother cat would never do that, so the cat is confused. It's better, then, to let the cat do its milk-treading until it is satisfied. You need to understand that your cat will always be a kitten in relation to you, and will carry out many kitten-like activities. Once you understand that, you can behave more like the parent cat that the kitten needs.

Ear language

Whoever heard of humans using their ears to talk? We don't use our ears for that purpose, of course, but cats do. Our cat Olivia is a very pretty cat, mostly white with black markings and gorgeous blue-green eyes. She seems to know how pretty she is, and often behaves in a rather stuck-up fashion. Not long ago, a huge black tom cat had the nerve to trespass on what Olivia regards as her territory. When Olivia saw the mischievous tom, her ears began to rotate so that you could see part of the back of them from the front. This was a very important signal to the other cat. It meant Olivia was likely to attack the tom if he didn't leave as fast as he possibly could! Ear signals are another means of communication that cats have but humans don't. Cats' ears can change direction when they listen to sounds coming from different places, but the ears also adopt special positions that indicate a cat's mood or intention.

Apparently there are five basic ear signals that cats use. They include relaxed, alert, agitated, defensive, and aggressive. When a cat is relaxed, its ears point forward and slightly outward, as it listens for things over a wide range. When it hears something interesting the ears change to the alert position, becoming fully erect with the openings pointing directly forward. When a cat is agitated, its ears begin to twitch. In some wild cats, like the lynx, this signal is even more obvious because this species grows tufts of hair at the ends of the ears. These tufts can wave about, giving a more pronounced signal. Some domestic cats, such as Abyssinians, still have a hint of this tuft.

In defensive mode, a cat flattens its ears against its head. This is a way of protecting them during a fight. Aggression is shown by rotating the ears.

I had seen Olivia adopt this aggressive signal, and it seemed to work. She had basically been saying to the tom cat that she was going to give him trouble, while at the same time saying she was not scared enough to flatten her ears completely. The tom looked at her for a moment then scurried away in the opposite direction.

The big cats in the wild communicate with each other in similar ways to our friends, the small domestic cats. The tiger, for instance, has its own variation on ear communication. It has a huge white spot ringed with black on the back of each ear. You certainly know when the tiger gets angry and sends out its warning, because the two white spots rotate into view. Other wild cats have ear markings that act in the same way.

Cat or snake?

Cats use more than their ears to give warnings of course. I often hear one of our cats hiss when it has been startled by an animal it does not know, or even by a visiting human. Desmond Morris, the expert on animal – including human – behavior, believes that the hiss of a cat and the hiss of a snake sound very similar, and that perhaps this is meant to be so. Predators have a lot of respect for poisonous snakes, and they will hesitate instinctively if they hear the hiss of an angry one.

The cat's hiss may have developed in order to make a predator hesitate for a moment, which might be just long enough to allow a cat to escape. It's also interesting that cats spit as well as hiss, which is another snake-like form of behavior.

Tabby cats might have developed an extra snake trick to scare off attackers. When a tabby lies curled up among rocks or trees, its colors and its shape make it look strangely like a coiled-up snake. Tabby markings may be deliberate imitation camouflage to put off potential attackers such as large birds of prey.

The disappearing cat

Millicent is a number one mother cat. In fact, she is the mother of all the cats that live with us now. We were very happy when Millicent was expecting her first litter, and we fussed over her quite a bit and generally kept an eye on her. The closer her time came the more we watched. Then, just days before she was ready to give birth, Millicent disappeared!

We knew that she would look for somewhere safe and warm to have her kittens, but we thought it would be close to the house. After a day or two we became very worried. What could have happened to her? Had she given birth to her kittens? The days turned into a week and we began to fear the worst. Then, during the weekend following her disappearance, I heard a gleeful cry and my wife came running into the house.

"Come and look," she cried, and led me to the base of a tall tree that grew near the front of our cottage. "Look," she said quietly, and pointed upward.

About nine feet above the ground, the tree trunk divided into three main branches, creating a hollow. My wife was pointing at this hollow.

"I can't see anything," I said.

"Look closer," she urged.

As I strained to look up, a paw poked out from inside the hollow. Then, to my delight, Millicent's head appeared then disappeared. I quickly got hold of a step ladder and slowly and quietly we climbed up and peered into the hollow. There, snuggled into their mother, were several tiny kittens, nearly a week old. Millicent had made her nest in the safety of the tree hollow and had only come and gone from it when she was sure she would not be seen. What a clever girl!

We left her alone from then on, just checking once a day that the kittens were where they

should be and that none had fallen out of the nest. Cats are not really birds after all!

About a week later Millicent and all the kittens disappeared again. It took us several days to discover them. This time they were on the bramble-covered roof of a small shed at the back of the cottage. Millicent had moved her family one by one from the tree nest to their new location, and she might well move them again. The mother cat uses her teeth to pick up each kitten by the scruff of the neck and carry it.

If she gets tired she may have to drag it. All the time the kitten makes itself limp and curls its tail between its hind legs to make itself as short as possible. This reduces the possibility of being bumped on the journey.

Wild habits

Many people believe that cats move their litters because the old nest gets dirty or becomes too small. But these are not the right reasons. You have to go back to cats' ancient ancestors to find the right one.

When cats lived in the wild, the mother cat brought prey back to the nest to get her kittens used to it. After about 30–40 days the kittens would begin to eat solid food, and it was this change in diet that prompted a change in housing. The first nest was chosen for its snugness and safety, which is why Millicent chose the tree. In the next few months of their lives, though, after their teeth had begun to grow, kittens needed to be able to bite and chew the prey brought to them by their mother. So a new nest was chosen closer to the food supply. In fact, Millicent's second choice wasn't that good as it had plenty of space but was not that close to a supply of food. After a while, though, she moved the kittens again to a spot close to where she was fed every morning. So, even though she did not need to move her kittens, as they would be fed anyway, she still behaved as all cats had always done. The old ways simply don't go away, despite domestication.

- Cats purr to communicate their feelings – and to tell you that they want something!
- Cats can make more than 60 different sounds.
- Domestic cats purr when they breathe out and when they breathe in, but lions and tigers can only purr when breathing out.
- When you stroke a cat's fur, to the cat it feels like the licking movements of a mother cat.
- When a cat rubs against you, it is marking you with its scent.
- Cats don't live in groups or packs with a head animal. Every cat thinks it's the top cat!
- Cats greet each other, and dogs too, by rubbing faces.
- When cats scratch furniture they are doing two things: removing worn-out parts of their claws and marking their scent.
- An angry cat rotates its ears. A defensive cat flattens them against its head.
- A cat can hiss, just like a snake.

CHAPTER 5

Whispering to Horses

Parsley was almost two years old when she met her first horse. She could cope with cats all right, but a horse might be a different matter. She was used to large grass-eaters, as she would often approach a grazing cow in the nearby field and nuzzle its nose. I'm not sure what the cow thought about this, but it seemed just as inquisitive as Parsley. So when Parsley spotted a horse being ridden in the field by our lane, she simply stopped and watched for a minute, then went on her way.

If dogs are man's best friends, then horses are not far behind. Ever since the first wild horses were trained, they have helped carry humans and goods across most of the face of the Earth. However, humans have not always treated horses well. This is largely because we have not understood their language, and how they communicate with each other and with us. Now this lack of understanding is beginning to change. A few people are working very hard to teach us new ways of working with and understanding horses. These people are sometimes known as horse whisperers.

Wild horses

Around 10,000 years ago, humans first started using animals to do work or provide food for them. Probably the first horses to be domesticated were the wild horses found on the great plains of central Asia, the ones we now call Przewalski's horse.

At first, horses were probably used just for pulling. But at some point humans learned how to train them and ride them. This was a real turning point in our history. We could now travel farther and faster with much less effort. No one knows who first tamed the horse and trained it for riding, but we know that people in southwest Asia rode horses over 5,000 years ago.

On the continent of North America, the horses left behind by the Spanish conquistadors became the American wild horses. In about

1600, the plains Indians in particular began using horses for hunting buffalo, and for war. The ways in which one tribe, the Cherokee, trained their horses is particularly interesting.

Catching horses

The Cherokee lived on the flat plains of the American Mid-West. There are few valleys and canyons in this region of North America, so driving horses into one in order to trap and catch them was not really an option. The Cherokee came up with a better and quicker idea. When they found a herd of wild horses, they used to follow the herd. They did not drive it hard but walked after it, for up to two days.

When they felt that the herd was ready, they would turn around and walk away from it. The Cherokee had already learned something about horses. The horses, rather than running away, would turn and follow. The actions of the Cherokee had a kind of push–pull effect. Then the Cherokee would simply lead the wild horses into large, specially built corrals.

The Cherokee had clearly learned what the horses would do. But why did the horses behave in this way? To answer this question, we need to look at the different ways in which horses communicate among themselves.

Body talk

In the wild, horses are very sociable animals. They generally live together in groups called herds, and have to be able to communicate well with each other in order to know what is happening within the herd. Most communication is done through body language. This is one of the ways that horses "talk" to each other. Sometimes it involves the position of the tail or the ears, or the opening of the mouth. When a horse's ears are laid back, for instance, it means trouble. It is a threatening sign, similar to the ear signs that cats make *(see page 67)*. Ear movement is also used to show respect for a more important horse, such as the head male of the herd. More important horses greet less important ones with their ears

forward. Less important ones greet more important ones with their ears back. Everyone knows where he or she stands in the herd.

Older horses, particularly females, use their own special language to "teach" younger animals. In the past, few horse trainers have taken much account of this teaching behavior. Yet you have to watch and try to understand horses before you can really see how they act with each other. Monty Roberts, perhaps the best known of the horse-whisperer trainers, grew to understand by observing horses closely, and what he saw excited him. He discovered that the two keys to horses' body language are the position of the body and the direction in which it is pointing. This discovery became one of the mainstays of Roberts' horse-whispering methods.

Horses behaving badly

The horse which looks after the herd at close quarters is not the head male, or stallion, as many people think, but is the top-ranking mare. It is her job to run the herd and to discipline the young horses if they step out of line. She can do this very effectively with body language. For instance, if a colt is behaving badly, kicking at other colts or disturbing fillies, sooner or later the mare will single him out. With her ears pinned back to show her anger, she will drive the youngster out of the herd. This is a useful punishment, as horses are "flight" animals, which means they run from danger. They do not like to be isolated, because isolation makes them an easy target for hunting animals.

The mare keeps the colt out of the herd by glaring at him, her eyes throwing out "laser beams" of warning. After a while the colt will tell her that he is sorry by walking with his nose close to the ground. Then, when she feels he has been punished enough, usually before dark, she allows him back into the herd. But that is not all. She then grooms him thoroughly to make him feel secure and a part of the group again. If the colt re-offends, as he is likely to do, the same process takes place until he understands that he cannot get away with such bad behavior. He is told how to behave just as effectively as any human would be if he or she stepped out of line.

The lead mare uses her body position to communicate her feelings directly to the offending colt. Standing head on, especially with head lowered to shoulder height and neck stretched out, is the aggressive "I'm not taking any nonsense" stance. When the mare faces

the colt head on, he has to stay put. Turning away and standing side-on exposes a horse's vulnerable parts and means "I'm friendly and won't harm you." It's a friendly and accepting position, almost like holding out your hand to offer a handshake. When the mare is side-on to the colt, he knows that he will be allowed back into the herd.

Eye contact
Eye contact among horses is another part of

their silent language. When the head mare is keeping the badly behaved colt out of the herd, she keeps a steely gaze fixed on him at all times. As long as her eyes are focused on his, he cannot return. Only when she lets her gaze drop will he know that he is forgiven.

Horse noises

Horses make a sound called a whinny. A short whinny is a warning, while a long one is a sign of happiness. Different kinds of horses make different sounds. Asian wild asses bray,

mountain zebras whistle while plains zebras bark. In the wild, one kind of horse does not react to the calls of another kind, although they sometimes do in captivity. So zebras don't really understand horse language, and horses don't really understand ass language! The main thing to understand, though, is that horses do communicate – and that's the key to understanding and working with them.

A local horse whisperer

While I was talking to an animal feed supplier one day, the conversation turned to horses. He told me of a horse whisperer called Gary Witheford, who lives not far from me. I jumped at the chance of talking to this man as I wanted to find out more about the process. I had already learned a lot from reading about Monty Roberts and seeing the films that have been made about him. But to watch a horse whisperer at work would be fascinating.

When I called Gary Witheford to talk to him about horse whispering, he was too busy to stay long on the phone.

"I'm working with a zebra," he said. "I'll be able to ride it in a very short time. People think you can't train a zebra to be ridden, but you can. I can do it."

After a short conversation we agreed to meet a few days later. I was stunned by what he said. Talking to horses, or training horses, in a short period of time is one thing. But training an untrainable zebra is another. Everyone knows you can't ride a zebra. But this man could!

Gary had worked with Monty Roberts in the United States and was gaining a reputation second to none for helping distressed horses.

"I don't think of myself as a horse whisperer," Gary said when we finally met. "I train and help horses with problems. I'm a horseman, plain and simple. That's how I think of myself."

For Gary, there was no mystery surrounding what he did. It was based on a knowledge of horses and of horse communication that was far greater than most.

At first we talked about the "old" means of communicating with horses, commonly called "breaking." It generally involves breaking the animal's spirit so it will do what you want it to do. Its aim is to make the horse obey its master, or rider. It is a cruel and unnecessary process, yet the same methods are still widely used today.

Wild horses are proud and clever animals. They do not take easily to being told what to do by humans. To train a wild horse, people thought they had to break the will of the horse and make it react to what they wanted, rather than what the horse wanted. What the horse wanted to begin with was simply to run away as quickly as possible.

Fight or flight?

A horse will normally take flight because its hoofs and long slender legs give it great speed across open ground, allowing it to run away from danger. This flight ability is the horse's most important defensive mechanism, which has developed over the thousands of years of its evolution. Other animals, such as lions, tigers, cats, and dogs, stand their ground and fight

rather than turning and running away. But they, like humans, are the hunters, the ones that eat meat. They don't need to run away. Horses don't hunt because they don't eat meat – they eat grass instead. So they didn't evolve sharp pointed teeth and claws. This puts them at a disadvantage when trying to fight against hunters. Horses needed a mechanism to help them survive – and that mechanism is flight.

Flight animals are quick and agile, but they are also supersensitive. They have to be able to start running at a moment's notice. They must be able to sense and react to danger immediately. When they sense or see something they are not sure of, their first instinct is to run.

"Sacking out"

Monty Roberts did not like the traditional methods of breaking horses, and Gary Witheford feels the same way. Horses do not need to be trained in the old way with whips and ropes. The training method that Monty Roberts hated so much was the method his father used, called "sacking out." Here's how it works. First, a head collar is fixed around the horse, often by funneling the horse through a narrow passage so the trainer can get close to it. When the collar is on, a rope is attached to it. Usually by this time, the horse is terrified. Next, a sack is thrown across the horse's back or legs. This generally makes the animal panic, and it kicks and lunges with all its might. The horse can become crazed with fear and may injure itself in the process. It has no idea what is happening to it. It cannot know the real purpose of the exercise.

This "sacking out" process can last for up to four days, and it has just one purpose – to break the horse's will and stop it resisting and wanting to run away.

In some cases, the next step is to tie up one of the horse's legs using a small rope attached to its neck collar. This further disables it and continues to batter at the will of even the most valiant horse. Sacking continues with the horse in this condition, until, little by little, the spirit and the wish to run away are driven out of the poor animal.

Next it is time to put on a saddle, but again with one hind leg tied. If the horse resists, the sacking out starts over again. Don't forget, by now the horse probably thinks its last days are up! Finally, the rider gets on the back of the animal, and with its fight gone, the horse gives in. It takes about three weeks to break a horse this way.

Many people now regard this process as cruel, although those who use it will say that the end justifies the means and that the horse ends up being well trained. But why does the horse do what it is told to do? It does it out of fear, nothing else. And so one of the best parts of a horse's character has been damaged for life – its pride.

Advance and retreat

Some people think there is another, far better way to train a horse. It is based on the push–pull effect used by the Cherokee Indians (see page 78). Monty Roberts has used it too, and it has become an important element of the training methods used by the horse whisperers. Gary Witheford spent two sessions showing me how a horse can be trained using this method, which is called "advance and retreat."

By looking at how the head mare and colt behaved when the colt was being disciplined, it is possible to see a pattern develop. The mare advances on the colt, then retreats. The colt follows her as she allows him back into the herd. She advances again, when he has mis-behaved, and again she retreats to allow him to come home when he has been suitably punished. All these movements and looks add up to a kind of horse language.

Horse sensitive

Monty Roberts' method of training horses requires a knowledge of horses' language – a language he would come to learn and use because he knew he could not treat horses in the same way as conventional trainers. Roberts studied, listened to, and tried to understand horses. He came to believe that a good trainer can hear a horse speak to him, while a great trainer can hear a horse whisper. What he means is that a great trainer understands both the sound and body language of the horse well enough to know exactly what the horse is saying and how to respond to it.

The horse whisperers' knowledge of this horse language allows them to do their own talking or, when it is more subtle, whispering. The horse trainer has to become as sensitive as the horses he trains. By talking to the horse in its own language, the training process becomes completely different. And, best of all, it means that the horse need never be scared or injured during training.

Top horse

One day, Gary took me to a round pen where he was working with a big chestnut stallion. It was a magnificent horse. The stallion certainly looked full of himself, snorting and running around as if he owned the pen. He was relaxed and having fun. Then he noticed another male horse in a field next to the pen. Immediately he began to whinny and snort and to run toward this horse. The stallion was challenging him. He was telling the other horse that as far as he was concerned he was ahead of him in the pecking order. If the stallion was number two horse, then this other one had to be number three. The stallion was number two because Gary was number one, just as I am the pack leader to my dog Parsley. The hierarchy system exists in the horse herd in the same way as it does in the dog pack.

The other male began to whinny back, but he was not so aggressive. Our stallion continued to rush up to the fence and show how big, strong, and fast he was. In the end he must have felt that he had made his point. Next, he began galloping around the pen again. Gary explained that the stallion was establishing his position of superiority. Now it was Gary's turn to do the same, but not in an aggressive or frightening manner. Instead he had to gain the stallion's trust and cooperation. Only in this way would the horse do what Gary wanted him to do – and do it willingly.

"I'll get the horse to move in a certain direction," he began. "Then I'll get him to change direction. Just cracking the whip will drive him away – will make him flee in other words."

First, he faced the horse square on and looked at him eye to eye. A horse will normally take flight, and stay away as long as the eye contact is made. It acts just as the colt did when the mare fixed him with her glare. A piece of rope, called a sash line, can be pitched at the horse, or a whip snapped, to encourage it to flee. The horse whisperer is telling the horse he wants the horse to flee, and that he talks the horse's language.

Gary did just that, and I watched spellbound as the horse reacted and moved around the pen in one direction, then in another.

Advance and retreat again

Gary explained that the horse was fleeing as intended. He was being pushed away, just as the naughty colt had been pushed by the lead mare. Now we had to see if the stallion would do what he wanted to do and return to be with his number one. As Gary approached the horse, he galloped off around the pen. Gary got him to move in the way he wanted, just as he had done earlier. He was making sure the horse knew who was in charge. After several runs around the pen the horse turned one ear toward his trainer to tell him he knew the trainer was there. Then he turned both ears forward. Next the horse began to make chewing motions with his mouth. He was saying "I am a plant-eater, I am not dangerous but just eating." This means the stallion has shown the trainer a certain respect – just as the offending colt did to the mare. Finally, the stallion lowered his head to just an inch or so off the ground, which means, "I don't want to flee any more. Can I come back and join up with you?"

At that point Gary stopped, took his eyes off the horse, and looked toward the horse's flank. At the same time the trainer began to turn away, offering his flank to the horse. This tells the animal that he is welcome to return if he wants to. Then Gary slowly walked away and a wonderful thing happened. Instead of keeping on running, as you might have expected, the horse stopped, turned, and looked at Gary as the trainer slowly walked away from him.

Joining up

The stallion had sized up the situation, decided he didn't want to be left out, and slowly began to follow his trainer. Gary did not look back at the horse, but kept himself turned away. When he stopped, the horse stopped just by his shoulder. I felt like applauding, but I just stood there with my mouth open. Then Gary turned and the horse started moving again. He repeated this action three times. On the second time, the horse seemed a bit reluctant.

"He's still going to try to show how independent he is, but he's not sure if that's what he wants. What he really wants is to be back in with number one," Gary explained.

Sure enough, the horse came round and decided to follow his leader. This process that Gary used so effectively is what Monty Roberts calls "join up." It is part of the horse language that Roberts calls Equus (the Latin word for horse).

Equus

By observing horses in the wild, Monty Roberts learned the different signs that make up the language of the horse. He believes that the key to this language is the positioning of the horse's body and its direction of travel. The mare, when disciplining the colt, squared up to him and pointed her head directly at him. The colt knew just what this meant. And he would continue to know, by the mare's body position, what she was telling him. As long as she stayed facing him, he stayed away. If she turned and showed him part of her flank, she was beginning to invite the colt back in again. She, in turn, would wait for his signs that said, "I'll behave and listen to you." He had to walk back and forth with his nose to the ground. When he showed his flank to her, he was asking for forgiveness.

Eye contact also proved to be important. She held him at a distance by keeping her eyes fixed right on him. If she removed them from him he could consider asking to come back to the herd.

According to Roberts, these signs are made regularly and each horse understands what the other is saying. This is the language of Equus. By trying to understand and use Equus, Gary Witheford was talking to the stallion in much the same way as you would talk to someone in a foreign language. The horse understood what it had to do to join up with Gary. It had to wait until he had turned away, which told the horse it was alright to come back – to join up.

The trust factor

From that point on, Gary had the horse's trust. The horse knew he was not going to get hurt, or to be made to flee for good. With the advance and retreat method the horse knew what was expected of him. Now Gary was able to make the horse change direction just by dropping his shoulders. The animal knew what was being said to it and reacted. It felt accepted and part of a team.

The next step involved putting a saddle on a horse that isn't too happy about the idea. This is a difficult job, but if the horse trusts you, and you can show that you intend it no harm, then the task is much easier. Gary took all the necessary equipment into the pen and laid it out on the ground. The idea was to let the horse see it and know that it was not harmful. The horse then stood still while Gary fitted the saddle pad and saddle, and then tightened the girth. The horse still did not have a rope around its head and yet it had allowed the saddle to be put on. That was pure trust. Now Gary backed off, squared up to the horse, and gently drove him off so he could get used to the saddle. The stallion took off around the pen bucking and snorting.

In a short time, though, the horse had slowed to a canter and began the usual licking and chewing signal that meant he was ready to come back again. Gary worked the horse around the pen a few more times and then allowed him to join up. He also soothed and stroked the horse to assure it that everything was fine.

Gary put the bridle on slowly, lifting it over the horse's head. He then adjusted the bridle and the stirrups, looped long lines through the stirrups, and worked the horse around the pen using them. He was trying to make sure the horse would follow the bit and bridle happily. Then Gary stopped the horse, adjusted the girth, and gave him some more rubs along his back and stomach. It was now time to put one toe into a stirrup and lift himself up. He allowed the horse to feel his weight and agree to his getting on. Then he lifted himself up and lay across the saddle while talking to the horse to reassure him. Finally he swung his leg over and sat in the saddle. He was riding a potentially difficult horse just 40 minutes after beginning to train him. It was incredible.

The idea of working with another animal instead of trying to dominate it is not an easy concept for humans to understand. We can barely do it with each other. But the horse whisperers, or at least the methods used by men like Monty Roberts and Gary Witheford, have taught us that horses do communicate, and that we communicate back to them. By understanding their language we can work with them in a much more rewarding, and kinder, way.

WHAT DO YOU KNOW?

- People first rode horses over 5,000 years ago.
- Horses mainly use body language to "talk" to each other.
- Older horses use body language to teach younger ones.
- In each herd, it is the top-ranking female who keeps the other horses under control.
- A naughty horse is pushed out of the herd until it tells the lead mare that it is sorry.
- Relatives of the horse, like zebras, do not understand the language of true horses.
- Traditional training methods involved breaking the horse's spirit.
- Horses whisper to each other.
- Horse whisperers train horses by using their own language – by whispering to them.
- The key elements of horses' language are the position and direction of the body.
- Horses also use eye contact to communicate their feelings.
- By using horse-whispering methods, a trainer can ride a difficult horse after just 40 minutes of training.

CHAPTER 6

Intelligence in the Sea

Sometimes when I am sitting quietly, I notice Parsley suddenly raise her head and look alert. She has obviously heard something. Yet try as I might, I cannot hear anything. The sounds she is hearing are probably too high-pitched for my human ears to pick up. Some animals use different-pitched sounds as part of their language communication. One such language that we can hear is that of a wonderful and very intelligent sea mammal – the dolphin.

Sonar dolphins

Animals such as dolphins are much better than humans at transmitting sound signals through water. They make a range of clicking and whistling sounds to help them find their way

underwater. These sounds are like a reflector beam that tells them the location of underwater objects. This natural sonar ability of the dolphin is called echolocation.

Echolocation works in the following way. Dolphins emit sounds of a particular frequency. Sound, like all energy, travels in waves, and the frequency of a sound is the number of waves that pass in a given amount of time. The sound waves from a dolphin bounce off any object in its path and return to the creature. In its brain the dolphin calculates how long the sonar beam has taken to return, and therefore how far away the object is. The dolphin also uses the beam to determine the object's direction, so that it won't bump into the object.

Most research into dolphin behavior has concentrated on their communication system. Dolphins make ideal research subjects, because they are naturally friendly and are quick to take part in experiments. In one experiment, dolphins were blindfolded with suction cups. They were able to use their echolocation system to detect even the smallest difference in the shape, thickness, and size of an object.

Family groups

Dolphins, of course, are a kind of whale. Like horses and wolves, dolphins and most other whales live in family groups. The closest-knit family groups seem to be among the killer whales, the largest of the dolphins. They swim in groups of around 17–18 animals. Bottle-nosed dolphins live in family groups of about 12. These family groups travel together with other families in schools, which may number between 100 and 1,000 dolphins.

Family groups consist of a dominant male, some females, and younger animals. Dolphins hunt together in their groups, but they also play together in them. They seem to know how to have fun and enjoy themselves, just like humans. This is a form of communication that helps to bond the group, just as it helps us to make friends and enjoy the company of other people.

Dolphins also help each other. If one dolphin is injured, others will use their flippers to keep it close to the surface so that it can breathe. This is another form of social communication.

Clicks and whistles

Echolocation is a kind of communication with self, which the dolphin has evolved to help it live in its particular environment. When dolphins communicate with each other, they use their own set of sounds – their own language. This noise language consists of a complex series of sounds called phonations. They are similar to the clicks and whistles of the echolocation system. The dolphin makes these phonations in air-filled sacs connected to the blowhole on top of its head (the blowhole is normally used for breathing).

Researchers have monitored the noise communication of dolphins. We know, for instance, that certain sounds are associated with certain situations. Dolphins make a particular sound when they are in trouble, although these distress signals tend to vary.

Cries for help

The worst thing that can happen to a dolphin is to find itself beached, for example after swimming into shallow waters. Although a dolphin has lungs and breathes air, when it is out of the water for any length of time, its body overheats and the animal eventually dies. No one knows quite why dolphins become stranded, given their ability to use echolocation to locate where they are and what is around them. The probable answer is that their echolocation system has been damaged or is malfunctioning in some way.

When a dolphin becomes beached, it does what humans do. It calls for help. Somehow these calls can be heard from a considerable distance, and are immediately understood by other dolphins. If a school of dolphins hears the call, they stop what they are doing and come to the rescue. If the stranded dolphin is lucky, it will be helped back into the water by the other dolphins. Sadly, rather than saving the victim, other dolphins sometimes become beached in the headlong rush to help.

This behavior shows us how close-knit a dolphin family can be. One day we may be able to break the code of the dolphin's language and learn what they are actually saying to one another. In the meantime, there is much that we can learn from these friendly and communicative animals.

Absent without leave

Our ability to communicate with dolphins has led to dolphins doing a very unusual job in the US Navy's Marine Mammal Team (MMT). The members of the MMT, the dolphins, are trained to swim away from patrol boats and search the ocean floor for mines and other large metal objects that might be of interest to the military. When they find something, they return to their handlers and are given a device to place near the object they have found. The device releases a tethered buoy that floats to the surface. Divers can then follow the tether down to the object and inspect the dolphins' finds.

One such dolphin, named Wenatchee, went

missing for about three days during a search mission in the Baltic Sea. His disappearance caused major headaches for the US Navy. If caught, suppose he was considered to be a spy! A search was carried out for the missing dolphin, but without success. Luckily he returned safely, and experts seemed to think that he had taken leave to sample the fresh fish of the Baltic Sea!

Whale song

Like dolphins, larger whales such as the humpback also live in close family groups, called pods. These magnificent animals have their own unique way of communicating with each other. They make an eerie singing sound that is known as the "song of the whale." Each group of whales seems to have its own version of the whale song, which helps to bond together the members of that particular pod.

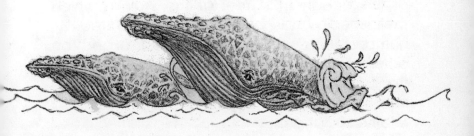

Whale song consists of roaring and groaning sounds, interrupted by shorter chirping and sighing noises. Humpbacks often repeat these sounds for hours at a time, particularly when basking in the warm waters of their breeding grounds. They also sing as they make the long migration each year between their breeding grounds and feeding grounds, although the composition of the whale song may alter during the journey itself. Scientists believe that the whales use their song to indicate their position to one another. Only the male humpback makes these sounds, so his whale song may also be some kind of signal to the female members of the group.

People who have listened to whale song remark on how beautiful and mystical it is. It seems to express the peace and harmony that these great creatures have achieved within their natural habitat. At other times, it appears to express the sorrow that these kindly giants of the ocean must feel at the way in which their species has been so badly treated by humans. Horace Dobbs, a world expert on dolphins, has remarked on the power and tranquillity that whales can exhibit. He has likened them to gods, and their dolphin relatives to angels.

Sea cow songs

One of the strangest, but probably one of the most endearing sea mammals, is the manatee. It is sometimes called a sea cow, because it grazes on plants on the sea-bed or river-bed. This strange-looking animal doesn't look like a very intelligent creature, but that is far from the truth.

Around the state of Florida in the United States, manatees are an endangered species. One of the reasons why they are endangered is because fast-moving power boats run over many of these animals while they are feeding or swimming. The manatee is too slow to get out of the way. In the early 1980s, a team of scientists from the Florida Institute of Technology decided that they would try to teach manatees to communicate warning signals to each other, to try to preserve the existence of the species.

Once the project started, however, the team found that the manatee already used a language of its own, which included nearly 1,000 different sounds. The scientists picked up both play signals and distress signals. The team then set about using computers and under-water sound equipment to try to decode the sounds. They sorted their findings into 13 categories, depending on the age and sex of the manatee, but they could not break the code. What the scientists did discover, however, was that the manatees' sounds related to moods and the sharing of inform-ation. When danger was sensed, the sounds seemed to intensify. This seems very much like the way in which dolphins use language, so there may well be a host of other animal languages that use noise as well as body language. But as yet we simply don't know about them. At any rate, the scientists' findings proved that the manatee may be slow but it is certainly not slow-witted.

- Dolphins make clicking and whistling sounds to find their way underwater.
- Dolphins give off a kind of sonar beam to stop them bumping into objects.
- Dolphins talk to each other by making different sounds through their blowhole.
- Dolphins will use their flippers to support an injured dolphin so that it can breathe more easily.
- When a stranded dolphin cries for help, other dolphins will come to the rescue.
- Specially trained dolphins help the US Navy to find hidden underwater objects.
- Whales make an eerie singing sound known as whale song.
- The sound language of the slow-moving manatee consists of over 1,000 different noises.

CHAPTER 7

Our Chimpanzee Cousins

Dogs and cats may play a much greater part in our lives, but chimpanzees are by far the closest animals to us in terms of their genes (the biological blueprints that make us what we are). In fact, chimpanzees have virtually all the same genes as humans – an astounding 98.4 percent.

As humans and chimpanzees are so closely linked genetically, it stands to reason that chimps should have some fairly sophisticated means of communication. Also, we should be able to communicate with them. Unfortunately, chimps' vocal cords do not work in the same

way as ours. As a result, communication with
them has to be through body language and
the silent language of signs, rather than through
our language of sounds.

Like humans, wolves, and horses, chimpanzees are social animals, and they too need
to communicate. When one chimpanzee finds
a large food supply, for example, it will hoot
loudly, jump about, and beat branches. This
behavior tells the other chimps in its group
to come and get it! Sound language is limited

to barks, grunts, and screams. However, chimpanzees can show a great deal about how they feel through their facial expressions. Like us, they can show fear, excitement, and anger. They use their bodies to send messages to each other, such as greeting another chimp with a hug or a touch.

Washoe

If chimps can communicate with other chimps by sending signals, then they should be able to communicate with humans in the same way. A famous chimp called Washoe showed just how much communication was possible.

Washoe had been raised as if she was a spoiled human child. She was brought up in a household in Nevada, in the United States. A scientist called Roger Fouts met Washoe and found that he was able to teach her to talk using sign language. The language he used is called American Sign Language (ASL).

When she was five years old, Washoe was moved from her home in Nevada to the Institute for Primate Studies in Oklahoma. It was the first time since she was a baby that she had seen another chimp. When Fouts asked her in sign language what she thought of the other chimps, she pointed to them and signaled,

"Black bugs!" It was the lowest kind of animal she could think of. Washoe was feeling superior. But imagine a chimp being able to express herself in this way. It shows us that humans are not the only animals to use language effectively.

Language, not speech

Before Washoe, a number of other chimps had been brought up in human households. Many learned to do things such as eating with a knife and fork, brushing their teeth, and using simple tools such as a wrench. But they all failed at one thing – language. What other people had done, however, was to confuse speech with language. In other words, they thought that only if a chimp could speak could it be said to have learned a language. What these people did not take into account is that the chimp cannot learn to speak as we do, because its tongue is too thin and its larynx is high. Also, the chimp is by nature a quiet animal. But it can learn language.

Washoe's adopted family, the Gardners, recognized this mistake and decided to use American Sign Language with Washoe. After all, chimps can do almost anything with their hands. In order to teach her, the Gardners used only sign language when they were with her. They wanted to give her a stimulating environment that would encourage learning and two-way communication.

When Roger Fouts met Washoe she had already learned a dozen or so signs. She patted her thigh to mean "dog," and she signaled "drink" by making a fist with her thumb outstretched. After about 10 months she began combining words to make sentences, such as "You, me hide" or "Give me sweet."

Washoe went on to astound the scientific world, and many other people, with her ability to learn and use a language. We cannot teach other animals such as horses to use sign language, but we can learn to use their language, and that is what the horse whisperers do. Likewise, I can learn to communicate better with Parsley and the cats by watching and listening to them. In this way I can try to understand how they communicate with other dogs and cats and with other animals, including humans.

The biggest primate of all

Another member of the family of primates, to which we humans also belong, is the gorilla. Gorillas are the biggest primates. They look terribly fierce and, when they open their mouth, show a set of frighteningly large canine teeth. In spite of these canines, gorillas are peaceful herbivores who live in tightly knit family groups.

One of the three main types of gorilla is the mountain gorilla, the species that the American zoologist Dian Fossey studied for so many years in Africa. In her book *Gorillas in the Mist* she describes her life among these wonderful creatures, and how she learned to communicate with them in the wild.

A family group of mountain gorillas is led by an older male animal, called a silverback.

Silverbacks have a very strong smell, rather like the scent of human sweat. They use this scent as a kind of communication signal to make others in the group aware of their presence. The scent attracts the female gorillas in particular, while making the younger group members take extra care to avoid upsetting the adults.

Super-purring

Out in the warm sunshine, when gorillas are feeling contented, they show their pleasure by making an odd purring noise. It sounds a bit like your tummy rumbling when you are hungry. This purring usually takes place when the gorilla is feeding or resting in the sun, and generally begins with just one gorilla. Once the first gorilla has started to make a noise, the others soon join in, creating a rumbling chorus. This sound is particularly important to gorillas as it shows which members of the group are nearby, and which ones are farther away. It is equally important in communications between gorillas and humans, as it allows unseen humans to show the gorillas that they are close by, and so stops any fears that the animals might otherwise feel. Humans aren't quite as good at making the sound as gorillas are, though!

The purr is a common form of communication within the gorilla group, but other sounds are used as well. A shorter purr is a telling-off sound. However, an adult gorilla will also use a type of pig grunt to make its feelings better understood when telling off its young. Silverbacks also use the pig grunt to intervene in squabbles between unruly youngsters.

Grooming is another form of communication

between gorillas. This is a social activity in which one gorilla meticulously cleans the fur of another gorilla. In this way the animals bond closely together, helping to keep the group united. It also helps to keep the gorillas clean!

WHAT DO YOU KNOW?

- In terms of their genetic make-up, chimpanzees are by far our closest relatives.
- Chimps use body language, particularly facial expressions, to talk to each other.
- Chimps also communicate by sending signals to each other.
- Researchers have taught chimps a special sign language to use when communicating with us.
- Gorillas are led by an adult male called a silverback.
- Silverbacks use their strong scent to let other gorillas know where they are.
- Gorillas make a purring sound, rather like the sound of your tummy rumbling.
- Silverbacks make a noise like a pig grunt to break up squabbles between unruly youngsters.

CHAPTER 8

Talking Is Good for You

In Ancient Greece the dolphin was a sacred animal. Its portrait was painted on pots and wall decorations, and its image was depicted on Greek coins. A Greek poet called Arion, who lived 2,700 years ago, described how he was saved from the sea by a dolphin after being thrown overboard by sailors. This tale from Ancient Greece is not the only account of dolphins saving humans. Perhaps it is in the nature of the dolphin to help other animals, as well as its own kind.

Today, swimming with dolphins is used as therapy for sick humans. People suffering from debilitating illnesses such as chronic fatigue syndrome have reported feeling happier and filled with renewed energy after swimming with dolphins. Even underwater wildlife photographers talk about their extraordinary feelings when swimming close to dolphins. They particularly value the eye contact that takes place with these communicative animals.

Some individuals claim that their lives have altered dramatically as a result of dolphin encounters. People suffering from depression appear to benefit from such experiences,

stating that the vibrations given off by the dolphins seem to pass right through their bodies. Sufferers claim that these underwater meetings renew their energy, get rid of their depression, and give them an understanding of things that they previously never understood. No one is sure quite how the dolphins have this effect upon humans. Do they set up a special energy field, or are they telepathic? The answers to these questions will come when we learn to communicate more fully with these marvelous animals.

It is not only communication with dolphins that can make us feel better and closer to the natural world. Dogs and other pets are often taken into hospitals, particularly children's wards, and homes for the elderly. In these places they can provide a much-needed focus of love and affection for the sick and the elderly.

Emotional animals

Some people think that animals do not have emotions similar to our own. Others, including myself, disagree with this idea. Animals show emotions at many different moments, and these are often very strong emotions too. Not long ago, I had to leave the house for a couple of weeks. As soon as Parsley saw my suitcase she knew what was happening. I could see the look of sadness in her eyes. Even her tail seemed to droop as she watched me prepare to leave the house. She showed just the same kind of emotion that a human might express in a similar situation. On my return, the greeting that Parsley gave me as I walked through the door showed beyond doubt that animals do have, and can show, emotion. She was so happy to see me that she could not contain herself as she skipped and jumped and licked around my face, all the time letting out little whimpers of joy. This was pure emotion.

Elephants are another species that exhibit their emotions very easily. Studies made of African elephants show that they are intelligent creatures that communicate mostly by sound. They make at least 25 different calls, each one with its own specific meaning. Some of these calls are rumbling sounds. An elephant calf, for instance, makes a hoarse, loud rumble when it is frightened, while a mother elephant uses a low humming rumble to make her calf feel better. Other sounds include screams, bellows, and roars.

The variety of sounds that an elephant can make shows that it has definite feelings and emotions, which are sometimes expressed in terrible circumstances. Young elephants in the wild have been photographed mourning their dead mother, killed by poacher's bullets. A young orphaned elephant, although still part of a larger family unit of around 12 elephants, will continue to show signs of the loss of its mother. It will often tag along at some

distance behind the family group, standing to one side when the other elephants are resting. It also shows signs of wariness of the adult females within the family. Male orphans will often leave the family group much earlier than the usual age of 12 or 13 years. Mother elephants are known to weep at the loss of a baby, or even a mate, and will often stand guard with other elephants over the body of a baby elephant for several days after its death.

Communication between humans is good for each and every one of us. Yet the most beneficial communication can often be between you and your own pet. And talking to animals is fun too! The secret of successful communication with our animal friends is to treat them with respect. You need to learn how they talk to you, and how you can talk back to them.

When Parsley greets me at the door after I have been away for a long period, I am left in no doubt about the real affection that we feel for each other. By her actions she communicates this affection far more easily and successfully than I can ever do with words. And that is what talking to animals is all about.

WHAT DO YOU KNOW?

- People suffering from depression and certain other illnesses feel renewed energy after swimming with dolphins.
- When dogs and other pets are taken into hospitals, they help to make children and elderly people feel much better.
- Many people believe that animals are capable of expressing emotions.
- Elephants make about 25 different sounds, each with a distinct meaning.
- Elephants mourn the loss of a parent or baby, often by weeping over the body of their loved one.
- The easiest form of communication is often between you and your pet.
- The secret of successful communication with animals is RESPECT.
- Remember, talking to animals is fun!